Why Should I Be The First To Change?

by

Nancy Missler

Koinonia House

Thank you for requesting this special "100 Huntley Street" edition of "Why Should I Be The First to Change"? May it be a blessing to you and thank you for your support of the Crossroads Family of Ministries.

David Mainse

Why Should I Be The First To Change?

Copyright 1991 by Nancy Missler

Published by Koinonia House
P.O. Box D
Coeur d'Alene ID 83816-0347
www.khouse.org

Tenth printing, January 2002

ISBN: 1-880532-70-0

All Scripture quotations are from the King James Version of the Holy Bible.

PRINTED IN THE UNITED STATES OF AMERICA

Table of Contents

Dedication

To my beloved husband, Chuck, for whom I would be willing to change a hundred times over in order to experience the depth of love, friendship and intimacy that we have now.

CHAPTER ONE

God's Ways Are Not Our Ways

Terror in the Mountains

We were at 13,000 feet somewhere over the Colorado Rocky Mountains. The turbulence from the violent electrical storm tossed our small blue and white airplane--that my husband was piloting--frantically back and forth across the sky. It seemed like hours that we had circled, trying to find a way out of the raging downpour.

Suddenly, we lurched to the right and headed straight downward! I tried to hide the panic and the overwhelming terror that consumed me. Our little plane spiraled downward, twisting and turning in the sky like a toy, corkscrewing to the ground.

My precious family--my husband, Chuck, my two sons, Chip and Mark--and I were flying from Los Angeles to Denver to meet some friends. When we encountered the storm, I begged Chuck to turn around. But Chuck had insisted that the thunderstorm was "no problem" and had stubbornly overridden my objections and headed into the clouds toward Denver.

Chuck and Chip sat in the front seat of the plane, while Mark and I were huddled together in the back. When Chuck realized that without oxygen we couldn't safely get above the storm, there was no other choice but to attempt to dive through it.

The storm was not our only problem. Chuck knew we had to land within the next five to ten minutes or we would be out of gas.

I have never in all my life been so petrified. I couldn't tell which way was up or which way was down; it seemed like we were spinning completely out of control!

The sky all around us was dark gray, except for an occasional lightning bolt that would brilliantly light up the interior of our little plane. Precious Mark, who was only ten at the time, was clinging to my lap and each time the lightning struck, it exposed his tear-streaked face. Finally he just buried his head in my lap and began to sob. That was all I needed. My own floodgates exploded within me and all the fear and terror cried out!

In my mind, I could see the newspaper headlines the next day: "Michigan family of four perishes in violent storm over the Rocky Mountains."

I never really enjoyed flying that much; I just wanted to be a "good sport" for Chuck. There had always been a trickle of fear within me, even when the weather was perfect. This time, however, there was no mistaking it--we were in deep trouble.

Sobbing, I cried out to God, "If You are really Lord and if You really do care and love me, then please, please, save us from crashing as I know in my heart that's what's going to happen. Lord, if You do save us, *I promise to give You the rest of my life to do with whatever You will*. Please, God, please...."

It seemed like only a matter of seconds, certainly not more than a minute or two, and we pulled out from under that horrible and frightening storm.

I could just barely begin to see. I could see mountain tops and trees only a few hundred feet below us, but thank God, they were *below* us! It was still raining, but I could now see the roads, the fields, and the buildings.

We crept along as close to the ground as we could, flying towards Colorado Springs where the control tower had said it was clear enough to land. Denver, it seemed, was still "locked in tight" with rain and fog.

A few minutes later, we landed in Colorado Springs!

I will never forget this experience as long as I live. God had truly heard my prayer. *He had saved us.* He had completed His part of the bargain. He was now going to hold me to "my part" of the bargain.

The next ten years of my life would prove to be the most difficult and painful ever, as God would lovingly "corner" me and make me faithful to do what I had promised Him that day in the plane.

Only Part of My Life

Up until the airplane incident in 1969, God had been only *a part* of my life. I was definitely born again and God lived in my heart, but He wasn't satisfied with that--He wanted more from me. He wanted the complete surrender of *my* life, so He could give me *His* own. As Paul says in Philippians 1:21, God doesn't just want to be "a part" of our lives, He wants to *be our very life itself.*

God wants us to know and to experience His own unconditional *Love*, not only for ourselves, but to pass on to others. He wants us to have His own supernatural *Wisdom* and discernment, so we can know when and how to love wisely. And He also wants us to have His supernatural *Power* and ability so we can live the Christian life as we are supposed to. In other words, God wants us to know and to intimately experience *His own abundant Life*.

However, it has to be our *own choice* to seek and to have this kind of life. Until that time, God will continue to be just "a part" of our lives.

Quite often, because He loves us so much, God will help us along with our decision by allowing situations into our lives that we, in our own strength, can't handle or control. He cares for us too much to allow us to remain stagnant. He, therefore, "corners" us, hoping that we will finally quit going our own way and choose to go His way.

God's Cornering Process

In Hosea 6:1 it says that God wounds us in order to heal us. For many of us this is a difficult truth to comprehend. It simply means that God loves us so much, He often allows painful circumstances into our lives. He knows that in the end, these circumstances will lead us to Him in a deeper way which, of course, is His desire.

A wonderful story by Dr. Haddon Klingberg exemplifies this principle beautifully.

A father and son were preparing to go on a camping trip. Their gear was lying out all over the living room floor, as the father was trying to organize it for packing. The little boy was looking over the equipment when his eyes stopped on the snakebite kit. He picked it up and said, "Hey, Dad, what is this for?"

The father put down what he was doing and gently explained: "Well, Son, if you were bitten by a snake, I would have to cut four small slits around the bite with this razor. Then I would have to suck out the poison."

The little boy had been listening intently, but when the father talked about the razor, his eyes got as big as saucers and he said, "Dad! Why would you do that to me? That would hurt so much!" The father lovingly responded, "*Son, if I didn't hurt you like that, you would die!*"

I think God, as our Father, deals with us in very much the same way. Listen to John 12:24-25:

"Verily, verily, I say unto you, Except a corn of wheat fall into the ground and die, it abideth alone; but if it die, it bringeth forth much fruit. He that loveth [hangs on to] his life shall lose it; and he that hateth his life [is willing to lay down his life] in this world shall keep it unto life eternal."

Jesus is saying here that only as we surrender and willingly lay our lives down to Him, will we ever be able to pick them back up and live them to the fullest. In other words, only as we become empty and cleansed vessels, will we ever be filled with God and His abundant Life the way He desires.

So, just because there is pain in our lives, it does not mean that God has forsaken us or that He no longer cares. It's usually quite the opposite. He loves us so much that He is trying to get our attention by "cornering" us. He wants us to stop going our own self-centered way and begin to live His Way of Love. By doing so, we will then, as John says, find our lives to the fullest.

God knows there are only two ways out of a corner. One way is to continue on in the way we have been going, following and *depending upon our own selves* (our own self-centered thoughts, emotions and desires) to meet our needs. This is probably one of the reasons we've found ourselves in the corner to begin with.

"There is a way which seemeth right unto a man, but the ends thereof are the ways of death [separation from God]" (Proverbs 14:12).

The other way is for us to yield ourselves, to set our own self-centered thoughts, emotions and desires aside, and *depend totally upon God* to meet our needs. Choosing to do the latter is the only way we will ever find the Love, the joy, and the peace we all so desperately need.

These two ways are totally opposite, and we can't follow both of them at the same time. We must choose.

"I call heaven and earth to record this day against you, that I have set before you *life* [which is His Way] and *death* [which is our own way], blessing and cursing; therefore, choose life, that both thou and thy seed may live . . . *for he is thy life*" (Deuteronomy 30:19-20 emphasis added).

Most of us want desperately to have God's abundant Life, but many of us are just not willing to go *His* Way in order to have it. "Any other way," okay, but not God's Way--not the cross, not total surrender, not death to self--that's too painful. We all want the easy way, the overnight solutions, and magic formulas.

God's Ways

I, personally, would never have chosen the ways God did over the next few years to bring me to that point of full surrender. But, again, God's ways are not our ways.

"As the heavens are higher than the earth, so are my ways higher than your ways..." (Isaiah 55:9).

In retrospect, however, after having passed through much of the fire and the refining process, I can honestly and truthfully say God's Ways have been and are perfect for me. As David said, in Psalms 119:71, "It was good for me that I have been afflicted, that I might learn Thy statutes."

And I *have* learned God's statutes. I *have* learned to yield and to surrender to Him, moment by moment. I *have* learned how to be emptied of self and filled with Him. He is *not* just a part of my life anymore, He has literally become my Life itself.

Looking back, the only thing I would change about God's cornering process in my life, is for me to have said "yes" to Him a little bit sooner.

Now, my story...

CHAPTER TWO

Too Busy for God

"Whitewashed Tombs"

In the early 1970s, just after the airplane incident, if you had seen Chuck and me, on the *outside* we might have looked like a fairy-tale couple. We had been married almost 20 years at this point with four gorgeous and healthy children, two boys--Chip and Mark--and two girls--Lisa and Michelle. Chuck had become a very highly successful business executive and we had a beautiful sprawling ranch house with a pool and stables. On the *outside* we looked like the "perfect family" who had everything anyone could ever want.

But on the *inside*, we were like so many people you see today: totally empty, unfulfilled, experiencing no real love, no meaning or purpose to their lives.

We were what the Bible calls "whitewashed tombs," which look beautiful on the outside, but on the inside are full of dead men's bones and everything unclean. The Bible goes on to say, on the outside you appear to people as righteous and loving, but on the inside you are "full of hypocrisy" (Matthew 23:27-28).

This is exactly what we were!

Back then (1969) the *Los Angeles Times* reported, "Marriage is a quiet hell for about 50% of American couples. Four out of 12 end in divorce, and another 6 (10 out of 12) are loveless utilitarian relationships to protect the children." I believe the statistics are even higher now.

Loveless Relationship

This loveless relationship is exactly what Chuck and I had. We had what I like to call a "professional marriage"--a marriage where two people are just *existing* together for the purpose of convenience, show, security, or as the newpaper article implied, "to protect the children."

What makes our story a little different than so many others you might hear is that we *were* Christians at this time. Not "backsliding" Christians, but ones who really "emotionally" loved God. After the airplane incident in my life and a similar re-awakening in Chuck's life, we began to teach Bible studies in our home; we went faithfully to church; we prayed daily; and we both became well versed in the Bible.

What was so sad, however, was that even though both of us were teaching others that Christ was the *answer* to all their problems (and in our hearts we knew and believed this to be true), in our own private lives, behind closed doors, this wasn't true at all. Our lives had become loveless and empty, just like the Israelites in Deuteronomy who were "just existing" in the land, never really "possessing" what was rightfully theirs.

The whole reason Jesus came was to give us His Life, His abundant Life--His Love, His Wisdom, and His Power. *Abundant Life, then, is simply experiencing God's Life through us*. God wants us to have and to intimately "know" this kind of life here, not only when we get to heaven.

Let me back up now and give you a little history as to how we got to this point in our lives.

Chuck's Background

Chuck has had a beautiful relationship with the Lord since he was about ten years old. His parents were both much older (his dad was 54 and his mom 43 when Chuck was born) so Chuck was "adopted" by a pastor of a neighborhood church. Pastor Hax took a personal interest in Chuck and became like a second dad to him. It was through this precious man that Chuck asked the Lord to come into his life and take control.

Whenever Pastor Hax had a speaking engagement out of town, he would always invite Chuck to go along with him. They would then have hours in the car to discuss their mutual love of the Lord. Chuck has been able to retain a lot of the information Pastor Hax taught him and has used it often, especially now as God has opened the door for a ministry of his own.

God knew what He was doing when He called Chuck to be His own. Chuck is the type that would never hesitate to tell anyone who asked about his beloved Lord.

In 1952, Chuck went to the Naval Academy at Annapolis. Even as a young midshipman, Chuck would share Jesus with anyone who would listen. He was totally "on fire" for the Lord. He was even asked to teach a pre-reveille Bible study (very rare at the academy), and in his senior year he wrote his term paper on Daniel's 70th Week Prophecy.

Blind Date

Chuck and I met on a blind date in 1956. We were "set up" by my best friend, Shar, who happpened to be Chuck's niece. When Shar and I were kids, she used to say to me, "Nancy, I want you to meet my uncle." I thought to myself, "Uncle? He must be an old man with a cane!" So I said, "No Shar, thanks anyway."

However, when we were in high school and Shar again said, "Nancy, my uncle is now in the Naval Academy. How about getting together with him?" I thought to myself, "Wow, Annapolis! Fantastic, a young man!" So I said, "Yes Shar, I'd *love* to meet your uncle!"

Well, I met Shar's uncle and I married Shar's uncle. So my dearest friend became my niece! And her mom, who was my mom's best friend, became my sister-in-law. (Chuck's half brother and my grandfather used to meet every week at Rotary and would often spend hours trying to figure out how on earth they were related. They never could work it out.)

Throughout our courtship, Chuck lovingly shared about his Jesus and all the wonderful things He had done for him. He also continually wrote me romantic love letters, calling me his "Proverbs 31 lady."

Because God's Love was becoming more and more real to me through Chuck, I became aware of how much I personally needed Jesus in my own life. I was raised in a wonderful, loving home, but

I still had an emptiness in my heart that nothing seemed able to fill. What I needed to know and understand (and the only thing that could fill that void) was the knowledge that God Himself loved me. In fact, He loved me so much that He died for me. He died so that I could live. I never understood exactly what that meant before.

As Chuck then shared with me and as I began to read the Bible, I realized, for the first time, that Christ had literally died for me *personally*. He died, so that I could be saved--saved from all my sin (all the many ways that I had offended Him). In other words, by my appropriating the "gift of Life" that He was offering and receiving Him into my heart, I could then be free--free from all the scars of the past and free to become *His own love child*. What an unfathomable Love gift and it was mine for the asking.

So, in May of 1957, I made the biggest decision of my life: I chose to give my heart to God. I asked Him to come into my life to be my Savior.[1] And He did.

Our Marriage

Three months after this commitment, Chuck and I were married. At that time, we were

---

[1] Acts 4:12; John 3:3-7

absolutely convinced that God had a fantastic plan for our lives together, because of the wonderful spiritual foundation He had already laid.

But let me tell you that many times in those first 20 years of our marriage as I saw that beautiful vision shattered, I'd go to God and ask, "What have You done, putting us together? It's a horrible mistake! We are so opposite and so mismatched!"

It's interesting because I hear so many Christian women today saying the very same thing. Recently one lady said to me, "Wouldn't God want me out of a marriage that is unhappy, and to marry someone with whom I would be happy and at peace?" (Actually, this lady already had someone in mind.)

I can now lovingly comfort these gals and say, "I totally understand what you are saying and where you are coming from because I have been there myself! I used to feel the exact same way. But, remember one thing. God never contradicts His Word,[2] so be sure it's God telling you to leave and not just your own hurt feelings motivating you to escape the pain."

---

[2] 1 Corinthians 7:10

I really believe that God wants to do a miracle *in us* and *through us*, even in the middle of our most painful circumstances. He doesn't want us to jump out of one fire and right into the next. We just end up taking the same "root" problems right along with us into the next situation.[3] Nothing is healed or solved, the situation is simply more complicated.

Too Busy for Church

Back to my story...

Shortly after Chuck and I were married, we moved to Colorado and began attending a church there. This particular denomination, however, lacked in-depth Bible studies, fellowship and prayer. So, without our realizing it, the excellent foundation we began with slowly began to erode away.

We were able to "hang on" to God for awhile. But without daily reading from God's Word, a consistent prayer life, and loving encouragement from other true believers, we began to fall away.

Someone recently said, "If you're not moving forward with God, you're not standing still, you're

---

[3] James 1:3-4

going backward!" That's exactly what happened to us.

Over the next few years (late 1950s and early 1960s), in our avid pursuit of Chuck's career, our enthusiasm and our love for the Lord seemed to get preempted by other "important things." We became "too busy" to go to church, to pray, to fellowship, or to read the Bible.

"He also that received seed among the thorns is he that heareth the word; and the care of this world, and the deceitfulness of riches, choke the word, and he becometh unfruitful" (Matthew 13:22).

We became, as this scripture says, "unfruitful." So the Lord allowed us to "be shelved" and "set aside" for 13 years until that airplane incident over the Rocky Mountains in 1969. How it must have grieved God's heart to see that enthusiasm, that potential, and that beautiful relationship He had begun in our hearts eroded away by apathy.

A Christian lady said to me recently, when I asked if she wanted to come to church or a Bible study with me, "Oh, I have many more important things to do!" That is exactly how we felt during those 13 years. We always had "many more important things to do" than to pursue getting to know God better or committng our lives to Him.

"Forasmuch as this people draw near me with their mouth, and with their lips do honor me, but have removed their heart far from me, and their fear [reverence] toward me is taught by the precepts [traditions] of men" (Isaiah 29:13).

Then the airplane incident happened in my life. And one year later, in 1970, Chuck happened to pick up a little book called *The Late Great Planet Earth* by Hal Lindsey. God used this fabulous book to absolutely blow Chuck's mind. The prophecies that Chuck had so long ago studied and taught at the Naval Academy were all right there in this book. And what excited Chuck the most was that so many of those prophecies, still future in 1956 when he taught them, were now beginning to happen right before his eyes!

I remember so vividly the night in 1970 when Chuck called from New York and said, "Nan, don't do a thing till I get home! I've got news that will absolutely change our lives. *I am convinced the Lord is coming back soon!* I know it sounds wild and I know it sounds preposterous, but it's true and it's all happening just as the Bible predicted."

Yes, the knowledge that Jesus would soon return was going to change our lives drastically. God had certainly gotten our attention now!

Giving Our Lives Away

In May of 1970, one year after the plane incident, Chuck and I and our two boys, Chip and Mark, recommitted our lives to the Lord and we began fellowshipping at a wonderful, love-filled, Bible-teaching church. We made many precious friends, and attended many Bible studies and prayer groups. Our enthusiasm was intense.

In those early days after our recommitment, I continually told God how excited I was to be living for Him again and how much I loved Him. I told Him *He could now do whatever He needed to do in me, to make me the woman of God that He desired.* And, of course, I meant this prayer with all my heart. However, I had no idea what I was really praying or how much God would require of me, in order to answer my prayer. (God is not satisfied with just "our words" of how much we love Him, He wants our actions to prove that love.)

So the next five to eight years of my life would turn out to be a series of unbelievable trials and tribulations--God's "cornerings" in my life--that I was in no way prepared or ready for.

CHAPTER THREE

Where's the Love?

Marriage Trials

Most of the struggles to come were from conflicts between Chuck and me.

I was raised by parents who gave their marriage relationship first priority. My dad was always there for my mom and her needs, no matter what they were. He was there for us kids, too, whenever we needed him. Dad and Mom always seemed to have a united front on all matters. I remember a very calm and undisturbed household with no internal tensions or outside pressures tearing it apart.

When I thought of marriage, then, Mom and Dad's was the kind I envisioned and hoped for. I didn't know any other kind existed. So it was a huge shock to find myself married to a "dynamo," who placed ten times more importance on time spent in his business and at work than time with me or the kids.

It seemed the tighter I would grab hold of Chuck to make him change and meet my needs, the more he would pull away from me and throw himself even deeper into his business.

At this time, Chuck was chairman of the board and chief financial officer of a major computer company. He "lived, ate and breathed" this company, thriving on the high stress and challenge of "growing" a big, dynamic business.

Chuck's typical workweek consisted of six 18-hour days. And, of course, he always brought home mountains of paperwork in the evenings and on the weekends. His secretary used to tell me he received between 40 and 50 important phone calls each day to return. It was an incredibly high-pressured job, but Chuck loved it.

Chuck also liked to travel. He was on the road (or more precisely, "in the sky") an average of one to two weeks each month. You can imagine the result of this kind of lifestyle--he had very little time for home and family. When he was home, with all the tremendous pressures on him, he would be totally preoccupied with the phone, the computer, business reports, mail, and so on.

When I complained about his long hours at the office or his extensive traveling, he would just respond, "Hey, that's what you married; that's what you're stuck with!" In other words, "Don't rock the boat! Don't try to change me!"

Chuck's Temperament

Chuck's temperamental makeup is entirely different from mine. He is probably one of the most intelligent individuals I have ever met. He has an I.Q. of well over 180. He is also an intensely charismatic person, both in his personality and in his conversation and he can captivate any size audience for hours. People are just fascinated by him, primarily because he is so articulate and because he has such a keen sense of humor.

However, Chuck also has intense highs and lows. Just when you think you are beginning to understand why he is acting and reacting the way he is, he'll shift to another gear and catch you totally off guard!

Knowing *when and how* to respond to him, then, is absolutely critical because if you are not sensitive to this, he can be very intimidating. Being tactful has, unfortunately, never been one of my strong points. I always seem to pick the wrong time and the wrong way to respond. And this used to get me into a lot of trouble.

Chuck's verbal abilities are incredible assets in the business world, but these same attributes can be devastating if you are on the other end of an argument with him.

I used to have the best "fights" with the bathroom mirror *before* or *after* actually confronting Chuck. In the bathroom I could always say "just the right things." But when actually talking with Chuck, face to face, it would always come out wrong or he would use a word I didn't understand and it would send me to the dictionary to find out what he'd just called me.

My Temperament

I'm not an explosive person. I have, in general, a rather placid temperament. But when hurt or attacked verbally, I used to *take everything inward* and allow it to stay there, to fester and grow, because I didn't know what else to do with it.

On the outside, I would smile and pretend everything was fine. On the inside, however, without realizing it, deep roots of bitterness and resentment began to grow and motivate most of my actions.

As Chuck would explode and hurl cutting remarks at me, I'd sit there, taking it all inward for future ammunition. Feeling extremely sorry for myself, I was completely blinded to any of my own shortcomings.

Then to get even with Chuck, I'd simply become a "martyr." For the next several days I'd give him the cold shoulder. I wouldn't speak to him. I wouldn't sleep with him. We were like the Israelites, who "just existed" in the land and never possessed what they truly owned.

It was at this point that I would go to God and ask, "Please tell me, what is the meaning of belonging to You when I am so miserable? I need Your Love, but I can't find it! *I've tried everything* I know of, but nothing seems to work. I'm reading the Bible. I'm going to church. I'm praying and I'm fellowshipping, but nothing seems to help. God, what's wrong with me?"

Diversity of Interests

While Chuck loves the fast pace and challenge of the business life, my favorite thing is to be home with my family. I like the "quiet life." Given a beautiful day, a sack lunch, and my Bible, I can amuse myself all day long, walking in the sun and enjoying nature.

I adore horseback riding. I love to gallop as fast as I can through the meadows with the wind blowing on my face, and imagine myself escaping off into the sunset. I love to walk in the forest or on the beach and meditate and talk to God. My dream has always been to someday live on a ranch or in the mountains. (God has recently answered that prayer.) Solitude, peace and a slow pace are very important to me.

Chuck, on the other hand, used to love the "hustle and bustle" of the city and, of course, the "wheeling and dealing" and the fast pace of business life. A perfect example: he would fly to Europe on a Monday evening (taking the "red-eye special"), speak the next two days in three different countries--being wined, dined, and hosted morning, noon, and night by several different international companies. Finally, he would again take the "red-eye" home Thursday night and be back in the office Friday for a full day's work.

Thus our marriage became more and more strained. Strained, not only because of our different outlooks, goals and personalities, but also because of business and family pressures and our dissimilar reactions to these pressures.

Different Stress Levels

Emotional trauma used to paralyze me, and often still does for awhile. I'm very transparent and carry my emotions on my shirtsleeve, so it's always been hard for me to hide what I'm actually feeling.

During this increasingly stressful time, my behavior clearly reflected my feelings. All I could think about was *my* misery, *my* lack of love, and *my* crumbling marriage. As a result I let my house go to pot; I let my kids fend for themselves; I didn't go anywhere or talk to anyone. I just stayed home, moped and felt sorry for myself.

Chuck, on the other hand--even in the midst of our most hurtful and anxious times--has always had the incredible ability to keep on going no matter what. He used to tell me he didn't "have the liberty to stop and feel sorry for himself." Chuck has an uncanny way of enduring pressure and to almost see it as "a challenge."

So again, after many more attempts to create a loving atmosphere for Chuck, I would finally just give up and quit trying. Why try? I felt it wasn't worth the trouble, the hassle, or the pretense. My efforts always seemed to end in futility anyway.

At this point I would again run to God and ask, "Where's the love You promise in a Christian marriage? Where's the abundant life that I'm supposed to have when I commit to You? If You really are the answer, then why am I still so unfulfilled? What's wrong with me? I'm miserable."

Other Struggles

From the first day I met Chuck, he has always had an insatiable drive to "be the best" at whatever he did. His job at this time was perfect for this intense drive of his. He took troubled companies out of bankruptcy, turned them around, made them profitable, and then would go on and do the cycle all over again.

Most of the companies he took out of bankruptcy were not just refrigerator companies or shoe stores, but "high tech" computer companies. So it was a huge responsibility with tremendous pressures. But again, Chuck seemed to thrive on the challenge!

We have *never* in our 38 years of marriage (maybe with a few exceptions at the very beginning) had an eight-to-five job with a stable income. We have either been millionaires (we've been there twice) or at the other end of the gamut-- totally broke and paupers.

The last few years of our marriage have probably been the hardest of all financially. We have literally *lost everything*. Three years ago we lost our beautiful "dream house," our cars, and our medical and life insurance through personal bankruptcy when Chuck's company failed. Then, two years ago, our rented home was on the epicenter of a 6.7 earthquake in California and we lost many of our own personal possessions. So, financially and materially, our marriage has been an incredible roller coaster ride.

When we were first married, Chuck used to say to me, "I can't promise you our marriage will be easy, but I do promise it won't be dull." Listen--he has kept that promise to the letter.

We have been married 38 years, and believe it or not, *we have moved 25 times*! (You heard me, 25 times!) Our boys used to say after another move, "Shall we keep our bags packed?" As you will see, our home life was never easy for our kids.

Chaos

Because of all the pressures at work, Chuck was often, understandably, on edge when he was at home. The least little provocation from the kids or from me would cause him to fly off the handle. He desperately needed peace and quiet when he got home, because his days at work were so hectic and stressful. This, however, we did not give him...

More often than not, we wouldn't know when Chuck was coming home for dinner, until he actually drove up the driveway. Even on the evenings he had planned to be home, his plans would often get cancelled at the last minute and he wouldn't show up. So, to our credit, it *was* very hard to plan for his arrival home. But, I'm sure we could have done a better job than we did.

The following is a typical "home-coming" scene. (Bear in mind, at this particular time we had four children and eight animals.)

Lisa would spot Dad as he was driving up the road. She would scream to Michelle, "Here comes Dad, quick put Annie [the dog] in the back porch so she won't bark!" Then she would yell to me, "Mom, Dad's home." I would shout back to her, "Where's Toto [another dog]?" And to Michelle, "Get Fluffy [another dog] off the couch--hurry up--put him in your room!" "Boys, pick up your bikes from the garage. Get your homework off Dad's desk! Quick, here he comes!"

In retrospect, I don't blame Chuck at all for being upset and for not wanting to come home; it really *was* chaotic.

Overwhelmed With Unhappiness

Sometimes my feelings of unhappiness over Chuck's comments or our situation would consume and just about suffocate me. They were like waves of hurt that kept breaking over me and eventually would drown me. I didn't know how to stop them from coming; nor did I know how to escape them.

I was sick to my stomach most of the time and often depressed.

I remember in 1975 being so overwhelmed with everything going on in my life that I locked myself in a darkened room and cried and cried until I literally thought I would burst. But then, because I didn't know of any other option, I pushed all the emotions down in my heart, locked them up tightly, forced a smile on my face, and came out to begin all over again.

I thought by burying my real emotions and putting a smile on my face, I'd eventually get rid of the anger and the bitter feelings. I thought they would just go away on their own and no one would ever know the difference. I believe the world functions this way, because it has no other choice.

Without Jesus literally taking our hurts away, as Scripture says, "as far as the east is from the west,"[4] we are *all* "walking time bombs" ready to explode.

The truth was when I buried my real thoughts and emotions, I never got rid of them. I only programmed them down deeper. And although I

---

[4] Psalm 103:12

didn't realize it at the time, those buried things just began to motivate all my actions.

Without getting rid of our hurts the proper way, by giving them to God and Him literally taking them away, we simply continue to act out of those wounds even though they are hidden.

Happiness Depends Upon Three Things

Ever since I was a little girl, I've always allowed my feelings, other's responses, and my circumstances to be a barometer for my happiness and to dictate my actions. I think this is natural for most of us.

If I could keep a lid on how I really felt, then everything would go smoothly for awhile and I would be "happy." Or, if I could control my circumstances and Chuck's responses, then I could give Chuck and the kids whatever human love (natural love) I had.

But if those feelings that I had never dealt with were triggered, or if Chuck said or did something hurtful, or circumstances occurred that were out of my control, then I would be miserable and not have any natural love or compassion to give to anyone.

A conversation I overheard at the Hollywood Bowl several years ago crystalizes the same attitude that I had.

A lady sitting in the box next to ours turned to her friend and said, "Well you know, I've come to realize that happiness is just the absence of tragedy!" She then went on to elaborate, "I'm happy when David is not in the hospital, when Shelly is not upset with me, when . . .!"

As I reflect on the early days of our marriage, I used to do the very same thing. My happiness and my ability to love Chuck depended totally upon how I felt, what the circumstances were, and what he had said or done to me that day. It seemed that my whole world rose and set with how *I perceived* these three things.

I Hated Being a Phony

More than anything else at that time, I remember absolutely hating being a phony. To me, a phony is one who says and does something on the outside that they don't mean or feel on the inside. And that's exactly what I felt I was being forced to do.

I knew the Bible was Truth. And over and over again it says in the Bible that we are to love God, and then we are to love others. The more I tried to do this, however, the more I would feel like a failure--it just didn't seem to work. I couldn't do it without being a phony.

Again I would go to God and ask, "Will You please tell me *how* I am supposed to do this genuinely? When I fake love or try to trump it up for Chuck, I feel like a hypocrite. And yet, *when I don't fake it, there is no love at all to give.* How am I supposed to love genuinely, as You say in the Bible?"

A Total Impossibility

I found struggling and striving to live the Christian life to be a total impossibility! How could I work up a love for someone whom I couldn't even respect anymore, let alone care for?

It grieves me because I see this same frustrated and despairing state of mind in Christians everywhere today. Such deep sadness behind smiling, "plastic faces," and I know, *I know* what they are feeling because I've been there!

God had to let me go all the way to the point of divorce before I finally surrendered and allowed Him to take off my blinders and show me the things *in me* that were keeping His Love (which was already in my heart) from penetrating my life.

Troubled Times

Our marriage over the next few years became typical of the ones we see falling apart around us today. Remember the marriage statistics: ten out of twelve marriages fail!

All of these marriages are frantically striving to find happiness, meaning and purpose for their lives in and through each other. Each partner is strangleholding and squeezing the other in order to receive the love and the fulfillment that they so desperately need. All of them are looking horizontally to each other to have their needs met-- thus, failure is pretty much assured.

I Wanted to Love Chuck

This is exactly what happened to us. I really wanted to love Chuck the way God wanted me to. I'm not a career-oriented person. Home and family have always been all that has mattered to me. All I've ever wanted out of life was to be a "good" wife and mother. But so often my *resentments and bitternesses* (that I had never dealt with), *Chuck's curt responses*, and our *continual stressful circumstances* would cause me to act just the opposite of how I wanted to act!

I understand how Paul felt in Romans 7:15 when he said, "For that which I do, I allow not: for

what I would, that do I not; but what I hate, that
do I."

Agape is God Himself

I had no conception at that time that God's
Love was any different from human love.   I
thought God's Love was poured into my heart
when I first accepted Christ, and all I had to do was
"name it and claim it" and His Love would be right
at my finger tips. I had no idea that *"Agape was
God Himself working through me. And that the
only way He could flow through me was for me to
give Him an empty and cleansed vessel to use.*

I believe many Christians today are just as
confused and bewildered as I was about God's Love.
Many don't understand, just as I didn't, that in
order for God's Love to flow at all, we need to first
be willing to surrender ourselves and set ourselves
aside. Remember John 12:24, which shows us that
in order to experience God's Life, we must *first* be
emptied of our own.

Another one of my favorite scriptures that
exemplifies this is 2 Corinthians 4:11: "For we who
live are always delivered unto death for Jesus' sake,
that the life also of Jesus might be made manifest
in our mortal flesh." Because this is not occuring
in many Christian marriages today (nor was it in

my marriage back then), God's Love *is* growing cold (Matthew 24:12).

CHAPTER FOUR

God, What Are You Doing To Me?

Our Children

Before I finish my story, I want to tell you a few things about our children, because they played a very important part in God's "cornering" process.

We have been blessed with four wonderful and beautiful children. Chip is now 35; Mark, 32; Lisa, 25; and Michelle, 19. Since they played such a prominent role in what God was doing in my life during those years, I must tell you a few details about them.

Our Boys

Everything seemed to come to a head the year we moved up north to the San Francisco area. Our marriage was just about over, Chuck's business had taken a turn for the worse, and we were having tremendous problems with the kids.

We had taken Chip and Mark out of their favorite high school in Southern California to make the move. They both hated the new high school and, of course, they became quite verbal about the whole thing. Chuck was extremely busy at this time, as he had just taken over another high-tech company and he was gone much of the time. Chip and Mark missed his companionship terribly.

Because Chuck and I were so embroiled in our own marital problems and preoccupied with our own circumstances and our own hurts, we unintentionally pushed the boys out on their own to fend for themselves. Since Chip and Mark found no answers, no consolation, and no comfort at home, they began to search for it elsewhere.

At this particular time, I was so consumed in my own problems that it was impossible for me to handle the boys' difficulties also. This was just another area that I could add to my already growing list of resentments against Chuck.

Lisa

In those days my Lisa was about six or seven years old. Being a very super-sensitive and quiet child, I know she just took everything inward that was happening around her, not really understanding it. As a result, she learned to build thick walls around her own heart, so that no one would ever hurt her the way she saw us hurting each other.

Now, so far you might say I had a few problems: my marriage was on the rocks; my kids were getting into trouble; and we were continually moving. But you still haven't heard about the situation that God allowed in my life that almost pushed me over the edge. God must have known I was a "very hard nut to crack!"

Michelle

My precious Michelle was born when I was 36 years old! She was the daughter I had prayed for and God had so lovingly given to me. Michelle, however, was born with extreme allergies and problems that evidently I had passed on to her during the last months of my pregnancy.

It seems when I was seven months pregnant, I "overdosed" on powdered milk (if you can do such a thing)! Since I knew that milk was excellent for the baby I was carrying, I figured, "If a little bit is good, then why not a whole lot more?" We also were watching our pennies at this time, so to me powdered milk seemed the most economical. I literally drank gallons of the stuff! During my seventh month, I developed a horrible allergic reaction and I was rushed to the hospital with painful hives and swelling. I apparently passed this milk allergy on to Michelle.

It's funny now, because I can remember sitting in our living room with a dear friend during my eighth or ninth month of pregnancy. I listened to her describe the agonies of having a baby who couldn't eat fruit of any kind because she was allergic to it and I remember thinking at the time, "How awful that would be! I sure wouldn't be able to stand that kind of trial!"

But God knew better. And in His perfect Love and Wisdom, He gave me a perfectly healthy baby, but one that was allergic not only to milk and milk products, but also allergic to the entire cow!

If Michelle ate or drank anything that came from any part of the cow--milk, butter, cheese, ice cream, meat, jello (which is from the hooves of a cow), or the long list of chemicals and by-products that also come from milk, like whey and cassein-- she would vomit uncontrollably and have diarrhea for days. She developed this allergy when she was about four weeks old and had it until she was about four years old.

On top of this allergy, when Michelle was eighteen months old, we discovered that she was hyperactive. My doctor suggested I try a chemical-free diet to control the hyperactivity. Some doctors believe that the chemicals in additives such as artificial colorings, flavorings, and preservatives, cause hyperactivity in children. These children have a chemical imbalance in their systems that causes an adverse or hyperactive reaction to these products.

So now, besides the diet of no milk, butter, cheese, ice cream, jello, and meat, Michelle could not have anything containing artificial flavorings, colorings, or preservatives.

It even got worse when we realized that she was reacting to the "natural" silicilates (the chemical in the additives) in apples, oranges, grapes, etc. Again I was advised to eliminate these from her diet. That left a diet of papayas, bananas, fish, lima beans, squash, spinach, and rice cakes! You try cooking for a two year old with that diet!

It was absolutely impossible! Michelle would see Lisa and the boys eating cookies and milk, cheese and crackers, candy and ice cream or just buttering their toast, and she'd cry to have some.

How can you explain to a two-year-old child, "Honey, the other kids can have some, but you can't!" There's just no way you can explain it! So she would just cry harder!

Chuck wasn't much help either. After I finally got him to come home for an evening and have a meal with us, he didn't have the patience to sit through all the crying and screaming, so he would finally get up from the table and leave.

In desperation, I tried feeding Michelle first and then locking her in her room when we ate. However, she knew exactly what we were doing--eating without her--so she would stand by the door and scream for hours until we came and got her. She rightly wanted to be with us as a family.

If I'd tried putting the whole family on the diet, which I did several times, the kids threatened to run away from home and Chuck said he would *never* come home!

So then I'd go back to just Michelle being on the diet.

It was an incredible ordeal, because I had to face this three times a day, every day for four years! I recently figured it out mathematically--I had to deal with this issue over 4,000 times in all.

I thought I would go crazy. Having a baby that is cranky, crabby, crying most of the time and unbelievably hyperactive every moment she was awake, literally tears you up and wears you out (especially when you are in your late thirties).

Michelle took only one nap a day and then for only about one hour. And for all those four years, she got up between two and four times every night, and seldom would go back to sleep.

[To show you the depth of this trauma, about ten or fifteen years ago on one of our trips to Israel, we stayed at a kibutz on the Sea of Galilee. The walls of our rooms were extremely thin and we could easily hear the people next door. One night in the middle of the night, I woke up in a cold sweat. A baby, down the hall, was crying just the way Michelle used to. I knew in my mind it wasn't Michelle, but all those years of stress evidently had taken their toll because I couldn't stop perspiring or shaking.]

As if I didn't have enough already, Michelle at age two developed a mysterious limp. One day she began to drag a leg. Thus, another group of doctors was consulted. At Stanford Orthopedic Hospital we were told that it was a deterioration of the bone marrow. They said if we ever wanted Michelle to walk again, she must be off her feet and in bed indefinitely.

Have you ever tried to keep a two year old in bed for any length of time, let alone a hyperactive two year old? I would tell Michelle, "Stay right there in bed and don't you dare climb out." She would look me straight in the eye, smile, and then as fast as she could, climb out. If I strapped her in, she would again stand by the side of the crib, scream, and never stop screaming.

All the other kids were raised with firm punishment for disobedience, and I believe in "spanking with the rod," as the Bible says. But if a hyperactive child cannot really help his behavior due to a chemical imbalance in their system, I would wonder to myself, "Do I continue to spank her over and over again for the same thing?" (There would be five or six offenses an hour. And I would have already spanked her three times the day before for the same offense.)

Continually, as I would watch her behavior, I'd question myself in my mind. "Did the catsup she had for lunch have food coloring in it? Or, maybe it was the toothpaste when she brushed her teeth? Should I spank her now? I've told her to stay in her high chair three times already and now she climbed out again. When I spanked her yesterday for the same thing, it was so traumatic. And it didn't do a bit of good!"

Just imagine yourself in my place. We had again just moved and now I was away from all my family and friends. I didn't have anyone to call to ask for advice or prayer. We couldn't find a home church where we felt comfortable. My marriage was on the rocks. My boys were getting into trouble. My Michelle was driving me crazy. It was the most excruciating time imaginable.

As if I didn't already have enough on me, Chuck would come home, see all the turmoil and say, "You really should get Michelle under control." (He thought she just needed more discipline.) Even little Lisa once asked me, "Mommie, should I act like Michelle so I can get more of your attention?"

I thought I would go out of my mind! I was losing control of everything I cherished. I knew God promised us in the Bible that He wouldn't give us more than we can bear. However, at this point, I was sure I was way "over the edge!"

Again, I'd go to Him and ask, "What are You doing to me? I pray and things seem to get worse. It seems like You have abandoned me when I need you the most."

Intolerable Situation

Chuck's business situation at this time was just about as tense and as difficult for him as the home front was for me. He didn't feel free to bring his worries or his struggles home, because he knew I wouldn't have a listening ear for him. In retrospect, it seems when we are so consumed in our own "self-centered world," it's impossible to see or even care where the other person is coming from.

I couldn't imagine that Chuck had as big a mess at the office as I did at home. I was totally oblivious to the fact that he had his own set of hurts and needs that weren't being met! Again, I was so preoccupied "with me," how could I have really seen what Chuck was going through or how to help him.

By all human standards, it was an intolerable situation. Both of us were locked so tightly in our own worlds of tension, strife, and trauma that "on our own" we never could have (or would have) moved toward each other. At this point, we had no love, no communication, nor any respect at all for each other.

Without God doing something pretty radical in both our lives at this point, it was a hopeless situation! We had sunk to that "professional marriage" level--just existing together.

During this tense time, if you can imagine, we still had our Monday night Bible studies in our home. We kept inviting people to come and share God's Love with us. But as our kids would often ask, "Why should these other people want what you two have? You're no different from the people down the street who don't even know God. In fact, our neighbors are probably kinder and more loving to each other than you guys are." Oh, how that hurt, because we knew it to be true!

I often wonder how many other "Christian couples" are out there, performing and acting as we were--sharing God's Word (knowing it's true and wanting it desperately) and yet, living totally loveless, empty, and meaningless lives.

Whitewashed on the outside, but inwardly full of dead men's bones. "This people draweth nigh unto Me with their mouth, and honoreth Me with their lips; but their heart is far from Me." (Matthew 15:8).

CHAPTER FIVE

Why Can't He Change First?

As I saw my marriage crumbling before my eyes, in desperation I tried anything *new* that others suggested might help. I was desperate for any new ideas, new formulas, or new methods to improve what I knew was dying.

"Read Any New Book"

The first way I tried to "fix" our broken marriage was to *read any new book on marriage* that came out. When I would find a new book, I'd say, "Great, here is the book that has just the answers for me; the perfect solution."

Basically, what I wanted was a magical formula I could apply and eventually it would change Chuck. It seemed easier at that time to take someone else's formula--someone else's answers--and apply them to my situation. I didn't have the time, nor did I want to take the time, to wait on the Holy Spirit to personally direct and guide me. However, when I got tired of performing or acting out that "perfect book solution," our relationship once again would falter.

Incidentally, the only way any of us can receive God's "perfect solution" for our own lives is by stopping and taking the time to listen to God for ourselves.

"God's ways are not our ways" and we can't simply take someone else's personal advice from God and apply it to our lives. All our personalities, temperaments and situations are different. What works for one relationship is not necessarily what God knows is best for another. We each need to seek the Mind of Christ and His specific Will from His Word for our own individual situation.

Of course this takes time, discipline and commitment, and at this particular point in my life, it was just easier to read a book.

I can remember a Saturday afternoon when I insisted that Chuck sit down with me on the patio to read a new Christian book that had just come out on priorities. I remember thinking to myself, "This will certainly straighten him out and show him how far out of line his priorities are."

How arrogant of me to think that way. What absurdity to believe that "I," with my little book, could change Chuck on the inside. That's God's job.

Look at my self-centered motivations. I wanted Chuck changed--not for his sake or for his best--but so that he could better meet my desires and my needs! God, however, knew my heart and my real intent. I didn't fool Chuck either. He didn't even hear what I read. How could he? God wasn't in it.

I've come to learn that real and lasting change comes about only in God's timing and in God's way, not in my own. It's an *inside-out* change that we want--a permanent change--not a temporary, *outside* change.

Inside-Out Change

I remember talking to one of my dearest friends who is a missionary in Bangkok, Thailand. As we shared, we realized that even though what God was doing in both of our lives (on the inside) was identical, His timing and His ways of accomplishing these things in each of our lives (on the outside) was totally different.

I live in the United States; I am married; I have four children; and my ministry is primarily to Christian women. My friend lives in Thailand; at present, she is not married; she has no children (at home anyway); and her ministry is primarily to third world unbelieving children.

My friend's circumstances and the people she ministers to are totally opposite from my situation and my ministry. And yet, the end result of what God is doing in each of our lives is exactly the same. Hopefully, we are both being conformed into His image.

"The Way of Emotions"

One of the most common ways we all try to have our needs met and our marriages saved is through the *way of emotions*. As women, we usually try this way first. It's the "natural" thing for us to do. We don't stop, think and respond, we automatically react and become carried away by the tide of emotion.

We must remember, however, that emotional outbursts always lead us deeper into the pits than when we first began, because we usually say and do things we never can take back. Of course, 17 years ago, I always lived the "emotional way." The following episode is a perfect example.

Cold as Ice

Chuck would call from the office around 7 p.m., after I had already prepared a nice dinner, and say, "I'm sorry, Honey, but I have to work late tonight. I'll probably be home around 10 or 11 p.m."

Immediately, buried feelings of rejection and bitterness, things I had never dealt with before, would be triggered and my composure would automatically fall apart. I couldn't control how I reacted; those buried feelings seemed to be right there, ready to explode at any moment.

Rather than act lovingly, as I really desired to do, my voice would automatically become as cold as ice. Even on the phone, Chuck could feel my attitude change. He would say, "Is everything all right, Honey? Is anything wrong?"

"No," I'd respond icily, "I'm fine!" And then I'd bang the phone down, absolutely furious at him. Anger, frustration, and hurt would totally consume me. My anger was really just a symptom of a much deeper cause (layers and layers of unvented rejection and hurt that had never been dealt with before, but simply buried).

All night long, rather than catch those negative thoughts and emotions, I would continually think about what Chuck had done. I'd entertain and mull over his actions again and again in my mind. This produced the horribly tense atmosphere that my poor Chuck would come home to later on that night. Looking back, it's a wonder Chuck even bothered to come home at all.

"Every wise woman buildeth her house, but the foolish plucketh it down with her [own] hands" (Proverbs 14:1).

I certainly was doing that--brick by brick!

"Controlling" my Feelings

When circumstances between Chuck and me were calm and I was able to somewhat control and hide my true feelings, things would go pretty smoothly for awhile. But when another shattering incident would occur, my "real" feelings and emotions would explode and, once again, they would direct all my reactions.

In retrospect, "controlling my emotions" simply meant covering them up tightly in my heart so that I couldn't feel them any longer. It meant burying them so deeply that I wouldn't be influenced by them anymore. When I did this, however, I also built a huge wall around my heart so that nothing at all--bad or good--could penetrate. In other words, I made myself hardened and insensitive to feeling anything at all! Thus, I not only prevented and "walled off" God's Love from coming forth through me to others, but I also prevented God from manifesting His Love to me personally.

[Note: Our heart is the area that God's Love resides in. Our soul is the area that our feelings reside in. When we become *hardened* because of sin (holding on to bitternesses, resentments, etc.), God's Love is not only blocked from coming forth from our hearts and flowing through us to others, but it is also quenched from flowing out into our souls where we can "feel" it ourselves.]

I heard a conversation on the radio many years ago that was troubling. A young man, a non-Christian, had called to ask the psychologist on the program what he should do with his real feelings over a tragic incident that had happened in his life. (I believe his wife had left him.)

He was repeatedly told by the psychologist on the radio program, "You need to get rid of your negative feelings, or you will continue to be hurt by this person in your life!"

Of course to this young man, getting rid of his negative feelings meant burying them deep in his heart, just as I had been doing. The young man kept responding to the psychologist, "I have. I've done as you say, but the end result is that I have become hardened. I have no feelings at all and it's frightening me."

I remember weeping, as this poor young man was told over and over again by this psychologist, "It's okay, you're doing the right thing. Keep getting rid of those feelings and you'll be okay." Again the young man replied, "Don't you understand, I have! I have!" Then in desperation he replied, "Tell me something, how do I do what you are telling me to do, and yet still feel love?"

It was so pathetic. I wished I had had the station's number, so I could have called in or done something for this young man. It was so tragic. But *without Jesus Christ literally taking our hurts away*--"as far as the east is from the west"--*we can't ever get rid of our pain*. Our only choice, then, is to bury it (as this psychologist advised) and, as a result, we "wall ourselves off" from feeling anything at all, even God's Love.

"The Way of Submission"

One of the other ways I tried to restore our failing marriage--and the way I absolutely hated the most--was *the way of submission*.

Ephesians 5:22, 25 and 6:1 summarize God's chain of command. "Wives, submit yourselves unto your own husbands, as unto the Lord ... Husbands, love your wives, even as Christ also loved the church, and gave Himself for it ... Children, obey your parents in the Lord."

This works beautifully in a family where everyone is committed to following God's plan of authority. However, when one or more of the members of the family are out of their place in that chain, or one member is not even a believer, then it has to be a totally supernatural act in order to genuinely submit at all.

Therefore, at that particular time, there was absolutely *no way* that I could have submitted and obeyed Chuck without tremendous resentment and bitterness. And, of course, that is exactly what happened.

In my mind, Chuck was the one "out of the chain of command." He wasn't loving me, so why should I have to submit to him? I felt as if I was being used and stepped on-- just like a "doormat." I felt as if Chuck could walk all over me and I was supposed to lie there and say, "Yes, sir. Anything you want." I absolutely hated it!

Now, there was no doubt in my mind that submission was God's Will for me. Over and over, the Bible tells us we need to submit to one another. So, on the "outside" with a big plastic smile pasted on my face, I would obey and submit to Chuck. On the "inside," however, I bitterly resented the whole thing. I resented not only Chuck, but I also resented God for making me have to put up with this charade!

There was even a period of time when I decided, "Okay, I'll submit to Chuck as the Bible says, but God never said I had to like it." So, again on the outside I would smile, obey, and say all the right words, but on the inside, I was screaming.

It reminds me of the little boy who replied, as he was getting scolded for not sitting down in class, "I may be sitting down on the outside, but I'm standing up on the inside!" That's exactly how I felt!

The problem was also compounded by my body language. Since our body language transmits 80 percent of our overall communication, if our body language is not transmitting the same message as our words, then our words will be totally discounted. Obviously, at that time my words and my deeds were not at all transmitting the same message, so this was a very short-lived solution.

I hated the way of submission and now I understand why. If we are working at submitting out of our own natural strength and ability and not God's, we *will* feel used and stepped on, just like a doormat. If, however, we can learn to set ourselves aside and begin to operate on God's supernatural Love and Power through us, then it will be clear that it's not us doing the submitting or the loving, but God acting through us. At that point, we'll feel more like "powerhouses" than doormats.

But I didn't know this back then. So again I'd cry out to God, "Is this what it means to love one another? How can I love and submit to a man who I don't even like anymore?" Talk about hypocrisy!

Matthew 23:25 describes it well: "Woe unto you, scribes and Pharisees, hypocrites! For ye make clean the outside of the cup and of the platter, but within they are full of extortion and excess."

That was me.

"Take any Class on Marriage"

One of the final ways I tried to save our failing marriage was to *find any class* on marriage or relationships: Any classes on how to "be a desirable wife"; how to "be a sexy mistress"; how to "be a beautiful mother"; how to "be an interesting partner"; or, how to "learn to do this or that...."

I'd sign up, go, sit in the front row and take thousands of notes. Then I'd go home and immediately try to put into practice all I had learned. Unfortunately, it was still just "me" doing the work, and not God through me, so eventually it would all fall flat again.

Some of the "play acting" that I learned in those classes was actually fun. In one of my classes, one girl had a great and unusual suggestion. "Nancy, get rid of all your kids for one evening and fix a fancy candlelight dinner. Then meet Chuck at the front door wrapped in nothing but Saran Wrap. Then seductively lure him into the dining room, and go for it under the table."

She had a great imagination and it would have been wonderful fun, if my heart had been in it and if our dining room table didn't have a pedestal right in the center.

Most of the implementing I tried, however, was tough, hard work. And it's no wonder, because again "I" was the one striving and trying to perform the Holy Spirit's job.

Just "hearing" the truths of the Bible and the principles of God in these classes did not, unfortunately, assure me that they would be manifested in my life. Without first letting the Holy Spirit accomplish His work in my own heart, making me an open and cleansed vessel, all the doing and the acting in the entire world would never make my actions genuine.

Just for a moment, in those marriage classes, I would see my true self as they would share God's Word. But when I came home, I soon forgot all that I had seen and, once again, I would try in my own power and strength to do what I thought I had just heard.

James 1:22-24 explains, "Be ye doers of the word and not hearers only, deceiving your own selves. For if any be a hearer of the word and not a doer, he is like unto a man beholding his natural face in a glass; For he beholdeth himself, and goeth his way, and straightway forgetteth what manner of man he was."

My love gestures to Chuck were not authentic, Love-motivated (I Corinthians 13) actions prompted by God's Holy Spirit. They were self-centered things I was doing to see if I could get Chuck to fall back in love with me, and thus meet my own desperate needs. In other words, it was just a performance or an act on my part.

The truth is, if we're not motivated by God from a pure and open heart, then there is no earthly way it will be God's unconditional Love flowing through us like I Corinthians 13. Only as we give ourselves totally over to God, as pure and open vessels, can He then love like I Corinthians 13 through us.

So again, the only thing that God needs from us is the willingness to allow Him to use our lives as open *conduits* to love others through. From start to finish, God must be the one doing the work, and not us! However, again I was unaware of this. So finally, just like all the other solutions, I would get tired of performing and give up, especially because I never saw Chuck trying.

Why Should I Be the First to Change?

I'd think to myself, "Why should I always be the one trying? Why should I do these things for Chuck when he doesn't even seem concerned about the situation?" In other words, *why should I be the first to change*? Why can't he change first?

I hear this question all the time now, "*Why should I be the first to change*? Why can't `so-and-so' change first?" Just the other day, even Michelle said, "Why do I have to be the first to say I'm sorry, he started it. It's not fair."

By worldly standards, it might not be fair. But as Christians we don't go by worldly standards, but by God's standards. And the reason God says *we* must be the first to change is simply that *our life depends upon it*! Our life depends upon our own willingness to allow God to change us and to conform us into His Image.[5]

---

[5] See 2 Corinthians 8:12

So it really doesn't matter who is the first to change, because God desires us *all to change and be transformed into His Image*. The faster we allow God to do this, the happier we will be.

So we must stop putting off what God desires and begin the process of being transformed. Being willing to change--being willing to surrender our lives so that God can live His Life through us--is the *only way* we are ever going to be happy and fulfilled and have that abundant Life we are all searching for.

A Diamond in the Rough

Once God brings us to the point of total surrender and we make the choice to go His way, then He can begin to *conform us into His Image*, which has been His Will all along.

"For whom he did foreknow, he also did predestinate *to be conformed to the image of His Son*" (Romans 8:29 emphasis added).

The process of transformation from our own image (where we express and show forth our own self-centered thoughts and emotions) into God's Image (where we express and show forth God's Love and Wisdom) is somewhat similar to the refining process that a diamond goes through to become the most beautiful gem of all. In the finished product, everyone can see and admire the Master's brilliant handiwork and His meticulous care and love. But the refining process itself is rough and most distressful as the Master gouges out and chisels away the rough spots and blemishes.

God's transformation process with us is very similar. He uses the trials and tribulations in our lives to break us of our own self-centeredness and our own self-dependency and to show us our own barreness and our need for change.

"Except a corn of wheat fall into the ground and die, it abideth alone; but if it die, [then] it bringeth forth *much* fruit" (John 12:24 emphasis added).

So, it doesn't matter who is the very first to change! God desires us *all* to change. And the sooner we do so, the sooner we can experience and pass on the Love and the Life that we were created to bear in the first place.

As we said earlier, *abundant Life is simply experiencing God's Life through us.* And this can happen in the trials and the bad times just as well as in the good.

The Real Problem

The real problem then was with me, not Chuck! The problem was in my *holding onto and burying* hurts, resentments, bitternesses, anger, criticalness, unforgiveness, judgmentalness, etc., (justified or not) *and not recognizing that these things separated me from God* and His Love.

God can't fill dirty, self-centered cups, and that's exactly what I had become!

"'Thou blind Pharisee, cleanse first that which is within the cup and platter, that the outside of them may be clean also" (Matthew 23:26).

Therefore, nothing in the world at that time-- books, classes, emotions, submission, etc.-- could have saved my marriage until I learned how to yield myself moment by moment to God, *love Him* and totally relinquish myself to Him. Then, and only then, His Life from my heart could begin to come forth and manifest the "real Love" that would eventually save my marriage.

CHAPTER SIX

What Other Way Is There?

Explosion Point

Our lives seemed to crescendo up to an inevitable explosion point and we began to talk of separation and divorce. Neither of us saw any other way out of the pain but to escape and run.

I think this is one of the reasons why there are so many divorces, split families and broken relationships today. Most of us don't know of any other way but to run from our overwhelmingly painful circumstances and unhappy relationships.

Our natural inclination is to get as far away as possible from the person who is hurting us or the situation that is causing us pain, and seek our fulfillment elsewhere. Since our "own" self-centered feelings and emotions are obviously directing our lives at that point, this is usually what we end up doing.

Most of us don't realize that as Christians we do have another option. We don't have to *vent* our real feelings, nor do we have to *bury* them. We have a third choice. We can *give them to God* and thus become an open vessel so God can love that other person through us.

But again, at that time, I was so totally consumed in my own hurt, bitterness, and resentment, I couldn't have made a rational or Biblical decision if I tried. I couldn't see beyond my own self-centeredness.

Since my own emotions were obviously in control of my life at that point, the only way "out" that I could see was to take the kids and leave. The only place I had to go was back to my folks in Los Angeles. So I arranged for a flight the following Friday.

Showdown

Two nights before the trip, however, Chuck and I began another one of our horrible arguments. Chuck hated these discussions, because we always ended up deeper in the pits than when we began. I, on the other hand, wanted more than anything else to be able to talk things out. As a child, I was taught to confront the other person, share my real feelings, and try to talk things through.

I have since learned that, yes, it is critical that we share how we really feel and what we are really thinking. But unless we share these things in God's timing and in His way (when we are open and cleansed vessels--full of His Love ourselves), nothing at all will be accomplished in either of our hearts except more frustration and hurt.

In my mind, however, this night was going to be different. I felt like it was my last chance to get through to Chuck, so I went into the discussion aggressively. In response to something Chuck said, I arrogantly replied, "But don't you ever want to hear what God wants to say to you?" I meant that if Chuck would just listen to God, God would show him how messed up his priorities were.

How presumptuous of me to act as God's little Holy Spirit nagger. He doesn't need me to criticize and badger Chuck. God doesn't function that way. So I fully deserved Chuck's response--it's one I will never forget.

Chuck simply turned to me and said, *"Won't you let Him.?"* (In other words, "If you, Nancy, would get out of the way, maybe I could hear God.") Those four little words are burned into my memory forever.

Well, I was absolutely shocked. I had always felt that I was the one who was "spiritual." After all, I was the one continually in Bible studies and prayer groups. I was the one reading God's Word and standing on His promises. And I was the one who had all my friends praying for Chuck. What on earth did Chuck mean that I was in the way of his hearing God? I sat back--absolutely stunned!

God used those four little words to blow my ears wide open. God wanted me not only to hear what He was saying, but also to see what was really going on in my own life: the pride, the self-centeredness, the unforgiveness, the bitterness, and the resentment that had covered over and quenched God's Love in my own heart.

"Why beholdest thou the mote that is in thy brother's eye, but considereth not the beam that is in thine own eye? ... Thou hypocrite, first cast the beam out of thine own eye, and then shalt thou see clearly to cast out the mote of thy brother's eye" (Matthew 7:3-5).

My eyes had always been focused directly on Chuck and the "speck in his eye" and I had completely missed "the plank in my own eye."

As I sat there, absolutely stunned, Chuck must have sensed an opportunity to tell me how he felt about us and our marriage and what he really desired in a wife. He seldom shared his deep feelings or hurts because he knew he would never have a listening ear in me. But this night God enabled him to share his heart as he never had before, and God opened my ears to finally hear.

(As you listen to what my precious Chuck said to me that night 15 years ago, picture your own husband talking and saying the very same things to you.)

Chuck began by telling me what he had always desired in a wife. "Someone," he said, "who is easy, warm and comfortable to be with. Where I can just be myself, and not on guard and defensive. Where the atmosphere is one of love and acceptance, not one of tension and judgment.

"Someone I can turn to for constant companionship and support, a teammate with the same goals and purposes. Someone who would love me just for myself, *not for what she wanted to make me into.*"

A Supportive Partner

Everytime I think back on that night in 1975, my mind always flashes back to Genesis 2:18. "It is not good that the man should be alone; I will make a help meet for him." Translated, this means a *help suitable for completing a man.* A help mate is not only to be loved and cherished, but also to unite with her spouse in accomplishing God's plans and purposes here on earth.

Deny it if we will, but a "help suitable for completing our husbands" is why women were created in the first place. We were created not only to fellowship with God, but to unite alongside of our men and in love accomplish God's objectives and His Will here on earth.

I don't believe we women will ever truly be fulfilled, until we learn to comply and fit into the mold we were made for in the first place.

It was interesting that Chuck never mentioned things that I would have thought to be important to him: a romantic and sexy lover, a stimulating and intelligent partner, a good mother and homemaker. I think, had I been graded on these, I might have fared better. No, what seemed the most important to him then (and now) was a "loving companion and a supportive partner," and these things I definitely was not.

Unknowingly, I had pushed Chuck farther and farther away by my self-righteous and judgmental attitude and my constantly pointing out his inadequacies.

The War Zone

Several years ago, I had the opportunity to fly home with a gentleman who shared Chuck's same desires in a wife. (At the time he was also separated from his wife and family for similar reasons.) Because I was teaching this material at that time, I asked him if he had anything to say to wives who were in circumstances like his.

He had a lot to say: "Tell them," he said, "men don't need another war zone at home. What we need is a refuge and a retreat from the battlefield." He said, "We have built up egos that we need at work. What we desire when we come home is a place where we can be who we really are without someone else telling us that we're a failure and we don't measure up."

This gentleman went on to say, "Tension at home just drives us to work all the more." This, of course, is the statement that stuck in my mind because this is exactly what I was doing to Chuck and exactly how he was reacting.

Chuck even has said recently that he had always desired a family and a loving home, because he never really had one growing up. He was an only child of foreign-born parents, and since his parents were more like grandparents than parents, he wasn't allowed to do the things other kids did and he was always very lonely.

All along, he said, he had wanted a wife and a family to fill that loneliness and emptiness. But with my constant bickering and griping, I had slowly eroded away his desire for a family. Then I turned around and blamed him for putting his business first.

Proverbs 19:13 is appropriate here, "The contentions of a wife are a continual dropping [like water dripping constantly]." This is exactly what I had been doing!

My True Self

As Chuck was pouring out these heart-piercing truths that Wednesday night back in 1975, I sat there stunned and inwardly began to cry. Chuck was describing the wife I had always wanted to be but knew in my heart I wasn't.

In all honesty, I hated the person that I had become. The acid of bitterness does horrible things, not only inwardly to our self-esteem and our self-confidence, but also outwardly to our countenance. There is a sourness, a hardness, and a harshness to the appearance of one who is consumed with anger and bitterness and unforgiveness.

That night God began to show me all the things in my own heart that were separating me from Him. He showed me the self-pity, the spiritual pride, the haughtiness, the self-righteousness, the hate, the unforgiveness, the resentment, the bitterness, the anger, the criticalness and the judgmentalness that I had stored up for years and never dealt with. These things then automatically quenched God's Life and His Love in me.

Separated From God

As God continued to reveal the awful truth to me, I began to cry uncontrollably. I had never seen my self-centeredness before in its true light. I asked God to forgive me for hurting Chuck so much. I had never seen it from Chuck's perspective before and I felt overwhelmed with remorse and sorrow. I confessed to God that I had held on to all those negative emotions and that, even though I didn't realize it at the time, it was sin and they had separated me from Him.

"Your iniquities have separated between you and your God, and your sins have hid His face from you, that He will not hear" (Isaiah 59:2).

No wonder God had been so silent in my life for so many years. He is Holy and He will make Himself known only to those who have a "clean hands and a pure heart [cleansed vessels]" (Psalms 24:4).

A New Way to Love

That night, even in the midst of all my emotions gushing forth, I was aware of the presence of God. He kept saying to me over and over again, "Nancy, I love you. I am going to show you a new Way to love--*a more excellent way to love*. Are you willing to trust Me?"

In my mind I responded to Him, "But God, I've tried all the ways there are. None of them have worked. *There are no other ways*." Again His response was, "I love you; will you just trust Me and choose My Way?"

Finally, crying out in my heart, I said, "Okay, God. I don't want to follow my own self-centered ways anymore, they don't work! I'm miserable! I'm willing to do anything You want me to do to change. I do trust You. I do love You. Please show me Your way of Love. This is what I really want to follow. And Lord, at the same time You are showing me this new way to Love, please, please change me into the woman Chuck is describing, because she is really who I want to be." (Little did I know at that time, that these two prayers were really the very same thing.)

This was the first time in 20 years that I had prayed "Lord, change me into what Chuck needs."

(Underlying all my previous prayers was, "God, change Chuck into what I need.")

This time I had prayed, "Lord, *change me first.* I am willing to become the wife Chuck wants because I see it's really what You want. You have free rein in my life to do whatever is needed. I give you my life to deal with and change as You please."

Finally, I had yielded my will and my life to God. Finally, I had kept my part of the bargain with God, not with just my words, but now with my life. It had been a long six years since the plane incident.

That Wednesday night in 1975 I finally yielded and relinquished myself totally to God. I gave Him all the things He had shown me that had separated me from Him--all the hurts, bitternesses, and unforgiveness. I finally gave Him an empty vessel to fill.

That night I gave God all I had to give, which was me! And you know what? That's all I am responsible for! I am not responsible for Chuck and what he chooses to do. I'm only responsible for me and what I choose to do!

Not a One-Time Choice

God impressed upon my heart that night, "Okay Nancy, I'll make you into the woman Chuck desires, but it will continually be your choice to either follow My `Way of Love' or to choose to go back to your own self-centered way of thinking. *Nancy, it's not going to be a one-time choice*: it's going to be a *moment-by-moment* choice."

Wouldn't it be great if we could only choose once and we'd be on our (His) way. Even if we could just choose once a day--like getting dressed in the morning--and we would be able to stay in that direction all day. But it doesn't work that way. To stay in God's Way, all day, is a *moment by moment process*.

God told me this over 15 years ago, and I bet I have chosen to go His Way over my own at least 100,000 times since then. No, it's not a one-time choice, it's a moment-by-moment choice.

As one girl said to me recently, "Nancy, it's not even a moment-by-moment choice, it's a second-by-second choice!"

Some gals in a recent retreat have coined those "moment by moment" choices as their "M and M's." They have made a big deal among themselves about it and kid each other continually by saying, "Are you still making your M and M's?"

However, be encouraged, our moment-by-moment choices do get easier the longer we walk with Jesus. The reason is that we quickly find out *there is no other choice* to make. When we don't make those right "M and M" choices, God's Life in us gets quenched and we go back to the pits where we started from and it's horrible. Take it from one who knows, there is no other choice!

"Yes, I'm Willing"

Notice, by the way, God didn't say to me that night, "Nancy, because of your choice, I am going to make Chuck into the husband you desire!" No, He said, "I am going to start with you, if you will let Me, and I am going to make you into the woman Chuck desires! Are you sure you are willing?"

My answer was again, "Yes, I'm willing. Do whatever You need to do to make me like You." (We often sing that song, but do we really understand what we are asking God to do?)

It had taken me 19 years from the time I first asked Jesus into my life to finally come to the end of myself, to die to what I wanted; to die to what I thought; and to die to what I felt. In other words, it had taken me 19 years to learn "to love God."

I never equated loving God with John 12:24-25. But this scripture is exactly what it means to love God.

"Except a corn of wheat fall into the ground and die, it abideth alone [have none of God's Life], but if it dies [learns to yield], then it will bring forth much fruit [God's Life]."

I finally began to understand experientially what I had promised God in that airplane incident some six years previously, when I chose to give Him the rest of my life to do His Will!

I had given my heart to Jesus 19 years before and I was definitely "born again." God had been in my heart all along, but "I" was the one preventing Him from coming forth and manifesting His Life and His Love through me, because I insisted on holding on to my own "justified" thoughts and feelings. These negative things then acted like a wall or a barrier over my heart, and prevented God's real Love from coming forth.

All of these things became sin *because I kept them, pondered them, entertained them, and mulled them over*, rather than immediately giving them over to God. These things then covered my heart and prevented me from experiencing His Life.

Psalms 119:70 explains it perfectly, "Their heart is as fat as grease."

When we sin--when we choose to hold on to our "justified" hurts, rather than giving them over to God--our hearts become covered, as this Scripture says, with a layer of grease. Then, absolutely nothing at all can get through.

Having the original, negative thought is not sin. *It's what we choose to do with that thought that makes it sin or not.* We have three options at that point: We can *vent* that negative thought; we can *bury* it; or we can *give it to God.*

If we can simply recognize the negative thought when it first comes in, acknowledge it, and immediately give it over to God, we have not sinned. We are still a cleansed vessel. If, however, we choose to hold on to that negative thought by either venting it or by mulling it over and over, it eventually will separate us from God.

"How Do I Do This?"

What I needed to learn then was "*how*," moment by moment, to yield and give God all my thoughts, emotions and desires that were contrary to His. Then I would be able to stay that open and cleansed vessel and His Life could continue to flow through me.

Since I was willing, God began to teach me *how to confess all my self-centered thoughts and emotions as sin* (i.e., acknowledge that I "owned" them and that they had separated me from God); He taught me *how to repent of them* (i.e., change my mind about following them and instead choose to follow His Will); and finally, He taught me *how to literally give these things over to Him*. (In <u>The Way of Agape</u> book and tapes we cover these three practical steps in great detail.)

My Responsibility

God, at this point, not only had a *willing* vessel, but an open and cleansed one to work through. Over the years since, I have found this is my only responsibility: *to stay a willing and cleansed vessel*.

God has all the Love I need; He has all the Wisdom I need; and He has all the Power and ability I need. I simply must be willing to allow Him to perform these things in and through me.

In the Old Testament when God initiated a call to His people, it was only after they chose to be "willing to be obedient" and "to do" what He had called them to do, that He made Himself known to them. And it's the same with us. God lovingly shows us what He requires of us, but it's only after we become willing to obey and to relinquish our total self to Him that He can begin to reveal Himself to us in a much deeper and more meaningful way.

So don't be like I was for all those years, waiting for God to do something or for Chuck to take the first step. You choose today to obey God (love Him) by willingly relinquishing your total self (all your self-centered thoughts, emotions and desires that are contrary to God's). In other words, give Him a cleansed and holy vessel to work through. He, then, will magnificently show you Himself and begin to work miracles in and through your life.

[Note: Remember, you don't have to *feel* willing, you simply must *be* willing. This is called a faith choice or a non-feeling choice. If you do your part, I promise you that God will do His. In His timing and in His way, He will align your feelings with the choice you made.]

"Let this mind be in you, which was also in Christ Jesus; Who, being in the form of God, thought it not robbery to be equal with God, But made Himself of no reputation, and took upon Him the form of a servant, and was made in the likeness of men; And, being found in fashion as a man, *He humbled Himself and became obedient unto death*, even the death of the cross. Wherefore, God also hath highly exalted Him, and given Him a name which is above every name" (Philippians 2:5-9 emphasis added).

CHAPTER SEVEN

A More Excellent Way

Teach Me about Your Love

I had finally opened the door of my life to God in a real and sincere way--I had not only committed my words to Him, but my life itself. He could now begin to transform me into His Image and show me what His Love was really all about.

Before this incident with Chuck in 1975, I had no idea that God's Love was any different from my own human love. I thought God's Love was simply poured into my heart when I first accepted Christ, and that all I had to do was claim it and use it. It didn't even cross my mind that *Agape was God Himself working through me* and the only way He could do that was for me to give Him an unclogged vessel to use.

[Note: *Just because we are Christians* and Christ dwells in our hearts by faith, *does not mean that we naturally or automatically have God's Love working in our lives.* We don't! We will always have His Love in our hearts (His Love will never stop flowing to our hearts);[6] however, it will not automatically flow out into our lives. *That, again, depends upon our own moment-by-moment choice.*]

So what I needed to learn at that time was how to recognize the things in my life that blocked and sealed off God's Love in my heart and how to give these things over to Him, moment by moment.

As I began to "take every thought captive," recognize the hurts, the anger, and so on, confess them as sin, repent of them, and give them over to God, God's unconditional Love in my heart began to permeate my being for Chuck.

My life began to change dramatically, from the inside out. I began to experience a new Love for Chuck that I had never encountered before, a new Wisdom to know how and when to love him that I never understood before, and a new Power and ability to live God's Way that I never possessed before. God truly had begun to teach me a "*more excellent way*" to live.

---

[6] See Romans 8:39

A More Excellent Way

Remember the example I gave earlier in this book when Chuck was late for dinner? Well, about a year later, after I had been walking God's Way of Love for awhile, a similar situation occurred. Only this time, I handled it in a much more "excellent way."

Chuck called one evening around 6 p.m. and said, "Hey, Honey, I have a free night and I'll be home by 7 p.m. Why don't you call the boys and invite them over for dinner and we'll have a great evening together."

"Terrific," I said. I was so excited! I quickly put a leg of lamb in the oven, called the boys at their apartments and told them, "Come on over. Dad's coming home early and we'll have an evening together." We rarely had dinner together as a family because Chuck traveled so much.

Seven o'clock came and went, and *no Chuck*! Seven thirty, 8, 8:30, 9 p.m., and still *no Chuck*. Finally, at 9:30 p.m., Chuck walked in the door-- genuinely sorry. He had met some "very important" businessmen as he was walking out of the office. They had all decided to go out to dinner and talk over some business matters. He was sorry, but he had just forgotten to call us.

Now my "natural" emotional reaction was still the same as it had been the year before.

[Note: Remember something very important. *Self-life* --own thoughts, emotions and desires that are contrary to God's--*does not improve with age*! No matter how long we have been Christians, our "self-life" will be just as ugly today as it was the first day we believed. *Maturity in Christ is simply the ability to recognize that "self -life" and give it over to God.*]

My natural reaction was to tell Chuck off. My roast was burned to a crisp, the boys and I had wasted a whole evening just waiting around doing nothing, and the girls had finally given up and had gone to bed!

By the world's standards, I would have certainly been "justified" to be very angry and upset. But God had begun to show me "a better Way," a "more excellent Way" to respond and to love.

All night long as I was waiting for Chuck, instead of being consumed in my own "justified" anger and frustration, I kept choosing as best as I could to give these things to God so I could stay an open and cleansed vessel for His Love.

I didn't simply bury my real feelings like I used to, or pretend they weren't there. I just kept recognizing them as they came up and verbally handing them over to God, thus allowing God's Love (which was already in my heart), to continue to come forth.

Let me tell you, it's hard work, constantly choosing *not to go by your own feelings and emotions*. But how excited and thrilled I was when at 9:30 p.m., it was *God's* genuine, supernatural, and unconditional Love that met Chuck at the door and not my own normal, self-centered reactions.

I genuinely felt no bitterness, anger or frustration over what had happened, because God had literally taken them all away. We were able to sit down and talk freely and openly about what he had done.

[Note: There definitely is a time to take a stand in God's Love and tell the other person how you are feeling. But we should only do this when we are cleansed vessels ourselves. Otherwise, we end up deeper in the pits than when we started. When we are cleansed vessels, the confrontation is done in God's Love. Then, not only will the lover be freed from presumptions and expectations, but also the one being loved will be prompted to respond from his heart and not his defenses.]

Chuck was so sweet and apologetic that night. I know he saw the "new" responses in me and I know he felt the peaceful atmosphere. We played games with the guys until midnight and had a great time.

The most thrilling part of all was that throughout the evening, I didn't have to be a hypocrite and trump up something I really didn't feel. God's supernatural Love came from my heart and it *was* genuine. This is what true abundant life is all about!

This genuineness and this freedom (not only for us personally, but for the people we are loving) is where, I believe, God wants us to live continually. Where our hurts, frustrations, fears and doubts are before Him, but where we are willing to sacrifice what we want, what we think, and what we feel in order for His purposes and His plans to be accomplished through us.

My Diary

Many incidents like this last example began to happen, as I continually tried to be that open vessel for God to use. My life became so exciting that I decided to keep a diary. (I recommend that you do the same thing as you begin God's Way of Love. Date the entries. Then, when times get rough, you can read them over and over and they will encourage you so much.)

Here are a few of my favorite entries from my diary during that time:

<u>August 1976</u> - (Three months after we had the "blowup" and God began to work so mightily in my life): "Chuck called today while away on a business trip and said, `Honey, the only thing wrong with our new marriage relationship is that it's no fun to travel anymore!'"

How many times I had pleaded, cried and begged Chuck not to travel so much. But nothing ever made a difference until "I changed" and allowed God's Love to become a part of my life.

<u>September 1976</u> - "Chuck has begun to come home from the office at noontime now, because he says he misses my company and wants to talk."

Chuck is a total workaholic. He would never take time off for anything. Also, he has always had a difficult time sharing his personal feelings until "I changed" and God's Love became a part of our relationship.

This last entry is the most precious of all...

<u>December, 1976</u> - "Chuck asked me today, If I were single again, would I marry him? He just wanted to make sure I was happy with what I had!"

There are volumes of examples of how God's supernatural Love began and continues to work in my life, as I stay an open and cleansed vessel for Him to work through.

To me, the climax of 15 years of living God's Way of Love happened only a few years ago.

We had gone to the Great Barrier Reef in Northern Australia for our anniversary. While on that trip, in a moment of quietness and intimacy, Chuck held me in his arms and read Proverbs 31 out loud. At each appropriate verse he called me His "Proverbs 31 lady." It had been over 30 years since he had called me that.

My whole life has now become a series of "out-of-the-ordinary," supernatural adventures! I am not just "existing" anymore, I am learning to really live--and live abundantly. By experiencing God's Life through me, I am learning to truly "possess the land."

Still in Love?

The Love that God has returned to our marriage and our family is incredible. During our early years of marriage, Chuck was never outwardly demonstrative. I think he just preferred that sort of thing to be done in the privacy of our home.

Now, however, Chuck privately and publicly shows me genuine and unreserved affection continuously. He has his arm around me all the time, caressing my neck and running his hand through my hair (even in church). And I can hardly keep my hands off him!

How wonderful in these hard and anxious times to have genuine love being expressed between two people who have been together for 38 years!

We were on a trip recently with about 15 other couples and many of them kept saying to us, "You can't have been married that long. You act like newlyweds!" They couldn't believe by the way we were acting, that we had been married such a l-o-n-g time. What a sad commentary on married life: the underlying thought being after you have been married that long, how can you still be happy and in love?

I pray our witness encourages and gives hope to anyone who sees us, that if God can return this Love to us, then He can do the same for them!

Focus on Jesus

When I stay that open channel for God's Love and I keep my eyes squarely focused on Jesus to meet my needs for love, meaning and purpose, then I am able to stop strangleholding Chuck to meet my needs.

I am also able to quit trying to conform Chuck into "my desired image" for a husband. I am able to simply accept Chuck as he is and genuinely love the "whole package."

There is so much freedom in this. I am *not* responsible for how Chuck thinks, what he says, what he chooses to do, or how he acts. I am totally aware of the areas that need changing and I will continue to pray earnestly about them. My responsibility is *not* to try to control and fix them, but only to *love Chuck as he is*.

However, the minute I stop looking to the Lord to be my confidence and stop being that open channel for Him, it never fails--I grab hold of Chuck and, once again, we both sink.

Loved Once Again

Of course, all this love and freedom has caused Chuck to totally "fall in love" with me all over again. I am now not only getting God's Love, as I remain an open and cleansed channel for Him to use, but I am also getting all the human, emotional love from Chuck that I ever desired in the first place.

I know, without a doubt, if it hadn't been for God intervening in our lives 18 years ago and showing us *how* to love with His Love, we would *not* be together today. God's Love has not only saved our marriage, it has also turned it around to where it is a hundred times better than it ever was, even when we were first married.

The Difference

Can you see the difference between how I reacted before and how I am responding now?

Before, I was frantically striving to live the Christian life on my own power and ability, on my own understanding of the situation, and out of my own self-centered human love. I had bottled up, quenched, and covered over God's Love in my heart, because I was hanging on to my own "justified" hurts, resentments, etc. Therefore, it wasn't God's Life (abundant Life) coming forth from me, but my own self-life. It's no wonder that I struggled so.

I was fabricating emotions and feelings that didn't exist, and burying the negative feelings and thoughts that did. My actions were totally motivated by those buried things, by the circumstances I was in, and by Chuck's actions. My eyes were always focused *on Chuck*, the situation, and on my own all-consuming hurts; never on God, where they should have been from the start.

Not only was I a prisoner of my own negative thoughts, emotions and desires, but I had also put Chuck into bondage because of my expectations and presumptions. It was an impossible situation and a vicious circle that neither of us could have escaped from without God's intervention.

Now, I can be genuine from the inside out because I am continually "taking every thought captive." I am continually trying to deal with those things that would cover my heart and quench God's Love. I am trying to stay that open and cleansed vessel, so it can be God's genuine, supernatural Love that comes forth from my life, not my own self-centered human love.

There is no more "play acting" on my part: I am yielded to God first on the inside so He can freely love His Love through me on the outside. It's God's Love that Chuck sees now. It's God's Wisdom showing me how and when to give that Love, and it's God's Power performing that Love in my life.

Remember, God always has plenty of Love, even for the unloveable. His Love is *not* based upon our feelings, our thoughts, or our circumstances, but only upon His faithfulness. So we can love like this not only in the good times, but also in the bad times even when we don't feel like it.

It's a totally freeing experience because what others see on the outside of me now is exactly what's going on on the inside. I am finally free to be the "real" me and yet reflect Christ!

The Key

I'm free as long as I keep my eyes squarely focused on the Lord and do what He calls me to do. Then it will be God loving Chuck and all the others through me. However, if I take my eyes off the Lord and go back to following my own self-centered thoughts and emotions, then again, it will be "Nancy" trying to love with her own human, natural love. As a result, of course, we all sink.

God's Love is not only the *initiator* of bringing the relationship back together, but His Love is also what *maintains* the relationship. God's Love is the *reconciler* of differences and the *foundation* by which all the other natural (human) loves can be rekindled, restored and allowed to grow.

As a result of God's Love being reestablished in our lives, Chuck and I are now not only best friends (natural, friendship love) again, but our physical lovemaking (natural, sexual love) has dramatically improved. After 36 years of marriage, we truly have become "one flesh."

Challenges

I don't mean to paint an idealistic picture here. My personality and temperament are still very much the same as they were 15 years ago and so are Chuck's. I am still super-sensitive, very emotional, and have a tendency to keep things in and Chuck is still very intense and explosive. We still have many challenges that confront us daily, but as we stay open and yielded to God, His Love can freely work through us and continually reconcile us. Our marriage is being healed, changed and conformed more and more into the relationship that God had intended from the very beginning.

Marriage, I believe, was originally designed as an earthly model of how wonderful our union with God could be. It was something we could see, understand and relate to, to show us how beautiful a relationship with God could really be. In the light of what we have done to our modern-day Christian marriages, however, it's no wonder that we don't know what God is like anymore! How grieved He must be.

God's Love--His true, genuine and pure Love-- has nearly disappeared from His people because they continue to honor Him with their lips only, but their hearts are far from Him (paraphrased from Isaiah 29:13).

Living Abundant Lives

To be authentic role models for our families and friends, so they will really want what we have, we must live genuine and abundant lives! I don't mean by having an abundance of things, lots of money, or important positions, but simply by having an abundance of God's Love, Wisdom and Power. By possessing *these* things (His abundant Life) we *will* be examples of what God intended the true meaning and purpose of our lives to be.

This is the only way we can prove to our kids and our families that what we have is worth everything to attain.

Please Forgive Us

I'm especially grieved for our Chip and Mark, who for years saw a mom and dad who "honored God with their lips" only. They witnessed the hypocrisy of our saying on the outside, "Hey, everything is great! God is wonderful! He is the answer to everything." Yet on the inside they saw us miserable, unfulfilled, and totally in need of genuine love. I ask their forgiveness and pray that our lives now are a genuine reflection of the miracle that God's Love can do.

Our precious Michelle has been totally healed of all her allergies, her limp, and her hyperactivity. I know God's timing is perfect. It's as if He waited to heal her until He had accomplished in my life all that He wanted to. Michelle now loves God with all her heart and she is constantly teaching me new things. We daily, thank God for her.

My sweet Lisa has grown into a wonderful woman of God. She has learned much, as she has watched God's incredible Love work supernatural healing and mending in all our lives. She is married now to Mark Bright, who, like her, is totally sold out to God. They both are a constant inspiration and encouragement to us.

No "Super Saint!"

Don't think for a moment that because I am writing this book, I'm some kind of a "super saint" and that somehow I have it "all together." I am just like you. *I am learning.*

However, I am experiencing something working in my life that is consistent, real and lasting, and something I believe many Christians never see or grasp at all. This is why I am writing.

Keep Looking Up

Remember, we can't change or control the circumstances that we find ourselves in; nor can we change or control the people that God has allowed in our lives; nor can we change or control our past (our failures); nor can we change or control the future and make it turn out the way we want. But, *we can keep our eyes upon Jesus*: by constantly denying ourselves and laying down our wills and our lives to Him. Then His Life and His Love can overflow into all our relationships and experiences of today.

I really believe with all my heart that there is no trial too big, nor any difficulty too hard that God's *Agape* Love cannot be the full remedy.

Of course, the question we always come back to is: Are you willing to have God's love and His Life flow through you like this?

I don't believe very many Christians will choose to go this way because it's *the way of the Cross* and it's costly. *Learning to love God is really learning to lose self.* And each of us must decide for ourselves whether we love God that much.

Are you willing to give God your total self--all your "justified" hurts, fears, doubts, anger, unforgiveness, etc.? Are you really willing to allow Him to conform you into His Image?

What Will Make Us Willing?

A girl from one of my classes once asked me, "I am not willing to go God's Way. What will make me willing?"

I asked her, "Are you happy? Are you content? Are you fulfilled? Do you feel loved where you are?" She screamed back at me, "Are you kidding? Of course not!" "Then," I said, "that (the pain) is what will make you willing!"

It's those hard, tough, perplexing, confusing, and painful corners that God so lovingly puts us in, that force us to be "willing to be willing"!

Truly, God has wounded me in the last 20 years, but in so doing *He has healed me and given me His Abundant Life.*

Only Way that Works

Why should I be the first to change? Because it is the *only way* to know His Love, His Peace, His Joy, and have His Abundant Life.

It doesn't matter if you have been a Christian seven months, seven years, or seventy-seven years! It doesn't matter how many Scriptures you know, how many prayers you say, how many Bible studies you lead, or how many books you write. It's still a moment-by-moment choice which is yours and yours alone to make that will enable you to have God's Life manifested through you.

Remember, *maturity in Christ is simply recognizing our self -life and quickly handing it over to God.*

God's Love Never Fails

Someone once asked me, "Well, Nan, how can you be sure this way will work? You tried all those other ways and they always failed! How about this one?" My answer to him was: "This way always works because this Way is <u>not</u> dependent upon my feelings, my understanding, the situation I am in, or the other person, but only upon God and His faithfulness."

This Way works even when I don't feel like trying, when I don't understand what's going on, and when the circumstances are totally out of my control! If I can just be "willing to be willing," that's all that is necessary. God will then do the rest!

I can honestly say that in the past 18 years since I have been walking this Way, God has never failed me. As I Corinthians 13:8 says, "God's Love never fails."

For almost 20 years, I was working right smack in front of God, totally blocking His Way. Now, thank God, He has put me into *His Way of Agape*--and let me tell you, *it's a much more excellent way!*

"Strait is the gate, and narrow is the way, which leadeth unto life, and *few there be that find it*" (Matthew 7:14 emphasis added).

Will you be one that does?

CHAPTER EIGHT

God's Way of Love

What is the Scriptural Secret?

Back in the late 1970s, when I began to share some of the miracles that God had done in our marriage, people asked me what the Scriptural secrets were.

I found it very difficult, however, to adequately explain what God had done "Scripturally." I could share the experience with them, like I've done with you, but I couldn't explain to them Scripturally why it had happened the way it did.

Each of our experiences are different and sharing our experiences by themselves--without putting the Word of God (God's principles) alongside--won't affect or change another person's life at all. *Only the Word of God will radically alter and change another's life.*

So I began to pray and ask God to show me Scripturally what He had done in my life. I wanted to share from His Word so other people's lives would be touched and changed. I prayed this prayer for three years and my study, *The Way of Agape* (God's Way of Love), was His answer to that prayer.

The Way of Agape

The *key* for me was--and continues to be-- implementing three truths in my life. This is essentially what *The Way of Agape* book and tape series cover:

1) Learning **what God's Love is** and how it differs totally from human love. Learning that most of us, even as Christians, are still functioning on human love and not God's Love at all. Learning that God's Love is *not* dependent upon our feelings, our circumstances, or other's responses, but that His Love is totally unconditional.

Then learning that **God loves us** with this same kind of unconditional Love. And that His Love is *not* based upon *what we do* for Him, but simply on *who we are* in Him.

2) Learning what it means **to love God with all our heart, will and soul**, and learning the difference between each of these terms. Learning

what quenches His Love in our hearts and *how* to yield, practically, these conscious and subconscious things over to Him so we can be free and God's Life can flow through us to others.

3) Learning what it means **to love our neighbors as ourselves**. Learning how we can put their will and desires above our own. However, the only way we can do this, is for us to *first* totally give ourselves over to God (i.e., love Him). Then He can enable us to love others, *before or instead* of ourselves.

The Way of Agape teaches us about a new way of Loving. A way of Loving that is totally opposite from the way the world teaches and probably totally opposite from the way you have been taught.

In *The Way of Agape* study, we don't learn *how to* give Agape, or techniques for appropriating God's Love, because *we can't learn to love like God*! Remember, only God is Love and we can't learn to be what only God can be! What we do learn, however, is *how to* yield ourselves totally to God. How to choose moment by moment to set aside our own negative thoughts, emotions and desires that are contrary to His, so we can become that open and *cleansed vessel that He can Love His Love* through.

1 John 4:17 says, "Herein is our love made perfect, that we may have boldness in the day of judgment; because as He is, so are we in this world."

And that is Love.

About the Author

Nancy Missler has been married for 44 years to Chuck Missler, an internationally-known executive, Christian author, and speaker. Chuck and Nan now live in Coeur d'Alene, Idaho and are the parents of four children: Chip, Mark, Lisa, and Michelle, and are grandparents to five: Mason, Emily, Noah, Madeline and Sommer.

Nancy has published three studies: *The Way of Agape, Be Ye Transformed* and *Faith in the Night Seasons*. Textbooks, Workbooks, as well as audio and video tape series are also available. These studies are the result of over 25 years of research.

Classes, Seminars and Retreats

Nancy has taught *The King's High Way Series* for the last 20 years all across the United States, as well as in Europe and Australia. Classes are also being held in New Zealand, Thailand, India and China. These taped messages (and their accompanying textbook, workbook and videos) can be purchased by writing or calling us at Koinonia House, P. O. Box D, Coeur d'Alene, ID. 83816-0347, or phone at (208) 773-6310, 1 (800) K-House 1. K-House Internet address is: http://www.khouse.org. Or http://www.kingshighway.org.

The Way of Agape - *Now on Video!*
RENT ALL EIGHT TAPES FOR ONLY $25!

Start a *Way of Agape* study group using videos of Nancy teaching! This series consists of eight one-hour video tapes and is available for a $25 rental fee.

LEADER'S GUIDE AVAILABLE

The Leader's Guide is available to help the leader of the small group review *The Way of Agape* principles and focus on suggested answers for workbook questions.

The Way of Agape Audio Set

By Nancy Missler

In this audio version of *The Way of Agape,* Nancy explains how understanding God's Agape Love has changed her life and how it can change the lives of others.

What is Koinonia House?

Koinonia House is a publishing ministry dedicated to creating, developing, and distributing materials to stimulate, encourage, and facilitate serious study of the Bible as the inerrant Word of God.

Chuck and Nancy have donated all their proceeds from these publications to this ministry.

A certificate for an initial year's subscription to their monthly newsletter has been included at the end of this book.

For more information please write:

Koinonia House
P.O. Box D
Coeur d'Alene, Idaho
83816-0347

or call:
1-800-KHOUSE1

On Internet:
http://www.khouse.org
or, http://www.kingshighway.org

$20.00 Value $20.00 Value

Certificate

This certificate entitles the person below to a full
year's subscription to *Personal* UPDATE, a newsletter
highlighting the Biblical relevance of current events.
(New subscribers only.)

Name _____

Address _____

City _____ PR _____ PC _____

email _____

Koinonia House Canada, P.O. Box 392, Cranbrook, BC   VIC 4H9